BARDSEY BOUND

BARDSEY BOUND

Enid Roberts

First impression: 2008

© Enid Roberts and Y Lolfa Cyf., 2008

This book is subject to copyright
and may not be reproduced by any means
except for review purposes
without the prior written consent of the publishers.

Cover design: Y Lolfa
Cover photograph: Aled Hughes

ISBN: 9781847710444

Printed on acid-free and partly recycled paper
and published and bound in Wales by
Y Lolfa Cyf., Talybont, Ceredigion SY24 5AP
e-mail ylolfa@ylolfa.com
website www.ylolfa.com
tel 01970 832 304
fax 832 782

Contents

Introduction

by the Right Revd Anthony Crockett, Bishop of Bangor

THE DIOCESE OF BANGOR is truly blessed in many ways, and not least in that it contains within it one of the foremost pilgrim centres of the Middle Ages, namely *Ynys Enlli* or Bardsey Island. According to the early 12th century Book of Llandâf, it is the burial ground of 20,000 saints. This may – quite literally – be an example of that cultic overkill for which the Middle Ages were noted. There can, however, be no doubt about the popularity of Bardsey as a pilgrim destination. It lies off the Llŷn peninsula; it is a truly frontier place, from which one still looks out and wonders about what lies beyond the horizon; it feels as if it is on the edge of another world.

In 1992, the then Bishop of Bangor, Cledan Mears, led a diocesan pilgrimage to Uwchmynydd, overlooking Bardsey, at the tip of the Llŷn peninsula. He was retiring that year and wished to bring the Diocese together, in an act which would be a tangible sign of the abiding presence of that great 'cloud of witnesses' who have gone before us in this wonderful place. As part of the preparation for the pilgrimage, Dr Enid Pierce Roberts wrote a series of articles in *Y Llan*, the Church in Wales' Welsh magazine. These became a masterly little book called *A'u bryd ar Ynys Enlli*. I remember reading it when it first came out in 1993, and it helped to kindle in me an interest in going on pilgrimage which has stayed with me ever since. It struck me at the time that a significant number of our people were impoverished by the fact that the original articles and the book were not available in English. I am delighted to be associated with this present translation, which will allow many more to appreciate the background to the pilgrimage to Bardsey. I hope they will be enriched by its presentation of the history and background of the pilgrimage. Like my predecessor, Bishop Cledan, I can think of no one more able to introduce this subject than Dr Enid. She is a scholar who has devoted her life to the study of the medieval Welsh poets, who for centuries served as the remembrancers of our nation. She also has the knack of wearing her scholarship lightly, so that we lesser mortals can gain access to their world.

When I was made Bishop of Bangor in 2004, I confess that there was one cause of deep disappointment which impaired the joy of being appointed to this, the most ancient geographical see in the Anglican world. I had arranged with the Bishop of St David's, where I was an Archdeacon, to have a sabbatical in 2005, when I intended to walk from Aries in the South of France to Santiago de Compostela in Galicia, Northern Spain. I had already, in 1995, walked from Le Puy to Compostela. My disappointment at being unable to take time off from my new post vanished when I became more thoroughly acquainted with the pilgrimage to Bardsey, for I walked from Bangor to Aberdaron below Uwchmynydd, in Lent 2005. The terrain and scenery are as beautiful as anything in France and Spain, and the history, with its outward and visible signs present in the ancient churches that mark the route, is equally as impressive.

The value of pilgrimage is enhanced by preparation, and I hope that this book, *Bardsey Bound*, will deepen the appreciation of the treasure that is ours, and help us all to feel the presence of those who have gone before us in the Faith, so that our pilgrimage will be a means of grace to us all.

+ Anthony

THE PILGRIMAGE PRAYER

I was glad when they said to me, Let us go to the house of the Lord; I was glad when they said to me, Let us go from the house of the Lord to follow the paths of the pilgrims of old.

God our Father, we thank you that they and we have been knit together in one, in the great family of your Church. Through the Holy Spirit grant that we may now tread eagerly in their footsteps, and through this pilgrimage teach us anew that we are the People of the Way, and that it is the way of Christ we are to walk day by day on the venture of faith. Let us perceive that there is a purpose to our life and a destination to our journey; for we dwell in tents but seek a city with foundations. Unite us as a diocese in one happy band of pilgrims; open our eyes, enlarge our horizons, spark our imagination, enrich our witness, sanctify our talents.

We bless your name, O Lord, for the beauty and tradition of Llŷn and for the ageless wonder of Enlli, the resting place of saints. As we journey, the sun will cheer us, the breeze will inspire us, and the rain will revive us. All things come of thee. So now let us take up the cross and venture forth. Let us set out with enthusiasm.

IN THE NAME OF CHRIST, AMEN.

R. Glyndwr Williams

Preface

O N 20 JUNE 1992, Bishop Cledan led a diocesan pilgrimage to Uwchmynydd, within sight of Bardsey, and five of us were privileged to cross with him to the Island of the Saints, to erect the cross, conduct a short service in the monastic ruins, and to present a copy of *Y Beibl Cymraeg Newydd* for the use of the island chapel.

These chapters, first published in the Church in Wales's periodical, *Y Llan*, were written as an introduction to the pilgrimage. Later, the editor and publisher of the periodical suggested they should be published in book form. This gave me the opportunity to add a little here and there, and thus the Welsh version, *A'u bryd ar Ynys Enlli*, was formed and published.

Bishop Anthony invites the whole diocese to join him, on 21 June 2008, in a pilgrimage to Aberdaron, where it is proposed to celebrate the Holy Eucharist on the beach. This book is a translation of *A'u bryd ar Ynys Enlli*, produced in the hope that non-Welsh-speaking members of a bilingual diocese will find it of interest.

If religion and superstition seem to be entwined in the accounts of pilgrimages, that is typical of the Middle Ages. The *Vitae* of the saints are a peculiar mixture of religion, history, myth, legend and folk lore of many nations, but as the historian Sir John Lloyd remarked, underneath it all there is more than a grain of truth. All knowledge was transmitted orally, generation after generation; it was the unusual, the supernatural, things that differed from the hard, monotonous, daily grind, that appealed most, and, naturally, the story teller often exaggerated.

I should like to thank many friends for their ready help: G C Owen for the illustrations pp. 29, 43, 47, 56, and the Revd. Canon Martin Riley for the drawing of Tywyn church, p.64. The late Dr B L Davies drew the maps, and the Revd. Canon Glyndwr Williams composed the pilgrimage prayer in both languages. The copies of the 'Possessions and Privileges of Bardsey Abbey', and the 'Absolution from Pain and Punishment' are published by kind permission of the National Library of Wales, Aberystwyth, and I thank the Venerable Archdeacon Elwyn Roberts for his help in deciphering and translating them.

Finally, I should like to thank Bishop Anthony for his support and encouragement, and for his kind foreword.

Enid Roberts

May 2008

Chapter 1

Bardsey Island
– Ynys Enlli

B ARDSEY ISLAND, THE REPUTED resting place of twenty thousand saints, situated about two and a half miles off the southern tip of the long arm of Caernarvonshire, known as Llŷn or the Llŷn peninsula, was a famous centre of pilgrimages in the Middle Ages. The English name conjures up no images, no impressions for the would-be pilgrim. The same place–name occurs in Cumbria and in West Yorkshire, the form Berdesei being found in the Domesday Book. The ending -ei / -ey is generally interpreted as island or higher ground, and the first part as the name of the owner, a personal name of Scandinavian origin. The same could be true of this little island since the north and west coasts of Wales, as we shall see later, were repeatedly attacked by the Vikings, from the end of the eighth century to the end of the eleventh century. No character of that name has survived in Welsh mythology.

On the other hand, the Welsh name, Ynys Enlli, the island (*ynys*) in tempestuous, treacherous waters (*lli* – current, the prefix en- emphasizing its strength) embodies the perils of the journey to this remote paradise. Even today, with better boats, fitted with engines, it is not always easy to cross to the island;

imagine the worry and peril in days gone by, in a light craft fitted only with oars and a sail. The mediaeval pilgrim risked his life on such a hazardous journey.

There is something mystical about its appearance, or perhaps non-appearance would be more appropriate. Those travelling from the north-east are denied a glimpse of the island until almost the very end of their journey on land; pilgrims from the south, on a clear day, will have caught glimpses of it on the far distant horizon, only to lose it again almost until they embark. What they all see is a steep, craggy mountain, rising sheer out of the water, making it impossible to see the land and dwellings beyond. Mediaeval people endowed Bardsey with a mixture of folklore, folk belief and ecclesiastical traditions, all of which would be related and discussed during their long trek.

About sixty years ago, the question was asked on a radio quiz, to what county did Bardsey belong, and the "correct" answer, according to the quiz master, was to Pembrokeshire.

This has been a long-standing popular belief in Gwynedd, but how and when it originated it is difficult to say. The earliest known written reference is in a letter Colonel Siôn Bodfel wrote to his uncle, Morys Wyn of Gwydir, 9 February 1647. When the monastery was dissolved, *c.* 1537, Bardsey became crown property; then, in 1553, Edward VI transferred the island and the abbey to Siôn Wyn ap Huw of Bodfel, Llannor, the Colonel's great great grandfather, for his good services at the battle of Norwich, where he was the king's standard bearer. In the days of the monastery, the island dwellers paid neither tithe nor tax, but when it became secularized the crown officials saw their chance. As the owner of the island, the

Colonel complained because tax had been levied against him, and insisted that Bardsey is not part of Caernarvonshire but of Pembrokeshire, or some other county in Wales. In a further letter, 7 April 1647, he complained that pirates continually visit the island, and since the island has to defend itself it should not have to contribute anything towards Caernarvonshire.

The Colonel does not mention that his ancestors, like most of the Caernarvonshire squires, had been in league with the pirates. Foreign ships landed on Bardsey, or anchored near the St Tudwal Islands (they never came to the mainland), and the local squires, including justices, the sheriff and the Vice-admiral who was supposed to be in charge of the harbours and havens of Anglesey, Caernarfon and Merioneth, went on board to buy their goods; all except Siôn Gruffudd of Cefnamwlch (d. 1584). According to Siôn Tudur's elegy, Siôn Gruffudd tried to stop the pirates and bring them to justice:

> Ni ddôi Sais yn nyddiau Siôn
> I dirio'n Aberdaron;
> Haws i ladron byrion, bach
> Hwylio i Bwll-heli bellach.
> Nis diengynt os dôi angor,
> Safai'n eu mysg yn safn môr.

[No Englishman in Siôn's time came to land at Aberdaron; it is easier for petty thieves to sail to Pwllheli now. They did not flee if they anchored, he stood among them in the sea.]

But what hope had he, when his own family defied him. In a case at the Star Chamber, 1569, his brother-in-law, Siôn Wyn ap Huw of Bodfel, was accused of being the chief supporter of the pirates. It was alleged that he always kept a servant on Bardsey, with a supply of food – cattle, sheep, bread and mead

– for the use of these visitors, and that in exchange he himself received wine, iron, salt and spice, and that the island was being used as a centre for distributing and selling the goods over a distance of sixty or eighty miles. Later, Tomas Prys of Plasiolyn was said to be doing the same from the St Tudwal Islands. The line between legal and illegal trade was extremely fine and vague.

But to return. It would be very interesting to know where Colonel Siôn Bodfel got the idea that Bardsey belonged to Pembrokeshire. Was it an old folk tradition in his day? Was it he himself who invented it, to avoid paying tax? Or was it the preoccupation and antiquarian learning of the time that invented it?

There was a tradition, or possibly a vague folk memory from very early times, of the sea overflowing and submerging land or lands in what we know as Cardigan Bay.

When discussing the age of the world, geologists mention that in some periods land sinks, causing new seas to be formed. That, of course, happened in primeval times, but even within the memory of the human race, when man was well established in Wales, changes on a small scale have occurred on the coastline in some places. Scholars agree that Ceredigion, some four thousand years ago, extended considerably further west. This extra territory would be flat lowland, not much above sea level; with an area like this it would be natural for the sea to encroach gradually. Another possibility is that, over a long period, the tide could have carried stones and silt, forming a kind of barrier or dyke that would keep out the sea; and sand dunes could form there. In such a situation, should storm force winds and a very high tide coincide, the sea could over-run, destroy the dunes and dyke and submerge part of the land – as happened in East Anglia in 1953 and on the Clwyd coastline in 1990. Today, it is possible to reclaim the land, but not so in early times; such submergence would be sudden and permanent. Naturally, the area lost at the time would be comparatively small, only a few homesteads at the most; but memory lingered on, and as the story was repeated generation after generation, it snowballed, until the few acres became a 'cantref', then a large, fruitful country with many towns.

The tale, as it is known to us today, tells how Cantre'r Gwaelod (The Lowland Hundred) was submerged. According to the present form of the legend, the land and its inhabitants were drowned because Seithennin, being drunk, neglected to close the floodgates in the dyke, and only king Gwyddno and his son Elffin managed to escape.

The remains of a very early story concerning the drowning of Maes Gwyddno (Gwyddno's Land) are to be found in a series of eight stanzas in the Black Book of Carmarthen, a manuscript written in the second half of the thirteenth century, but the stanzas could be several centuries earlier. One gathers from these that it was Mererid, the maiden in charge of the well, who was responsible for the catastrophe. The author calls on Seithennin to look at the destruction, but who he was and what his status was are not revealed.

In the seventeenth century, travellers returning from the Low Countries reported how the sea encroached on the land and how the inhabitants built dykes to try to contain it. Possibly that is what gave Robert Vaughan (1592?-1667), the antiquarian from Hengwrt, near Dolgellau, the idea that Sarn Badrig, the ridge of natural rock running out to the sea near Harlech, was part of a similar dyke. This would be about the time Colonel Siôn Bodfel was writing to his uncle.

Lewis Morris (1701-65) accepted the dyke, and, as an experienced engineer, he added floodgates, and stated it was because of the drunkenness of the gatekeeper that they were not closed against the tide. In a series of Triads written by Iolo Morganwg at the end of the eighteenth century, Seithennin is referred to as one of the Chief Drunkards of the Isle of Britain because, while drunk, he let in the sea over Cantre'r Gwaelod. In *The Cambrian Biography* (1803), William Owen Pughe stated that Seithennin was the drunkard who neglected to close the floodgates.

By the early nineteenth century, the story of Cantre'r Gwaelod was complete. It appealed to the imagination of Welsh and English writers, and, unfortunately, it was accepted by some historians and antiquarians.

In a paper, 'Cantre'r Gwaelod or the Lowland Hundred', read to the Society of Welsh Archaeologists at Caernarfon, 1849, the Revd Griffith Edwards, MA (curate of Llangollen at the time, later 'Gutyn Padarn', FRHS, rector of Llangadfan (1863-92) stated, 'Bardsey Island at one time belonged to Pembrokeshire and paid its taxes to it, amongst others, a county rate of four pence.' The same statement appears in his extensive introduction to his English ode, 'The Inundation of Cantre'r Gwaelod or the Lowland Hundred', in his collected works, published in 1895, where he states that the lost land extended from Bardsey to Ramsey Island. Unfortunately, he does not state the source of his information.

At the Haverfordwest meeting of the same Society, 1864, a letter was read from Mr Griffiths, rector of Merthyr Tudful, drawing attention to the special circumstances on Bardsey Island. 'Until now it has been *extra parochial*; there is no place of worship belonging to the Church of England on the island, and now it is in danger of being made part of Aberdaron parish and forced to pay the taxes of that parish.' He was eager to build a church on the island, and since it was to Pembrokeshire that it belonged at one time the matter should be put before the meeting at Haverfordwest. He would contribute £10 to a church building fund. His proposal received no support; it was totally rejected.

A few years ago a friend mentioned how the Caernarvonshire Education Committee in the 1930s, relying on this old tradition, requested from the Pembrokeshire Education Committee financial help towards maintaining a schoolmaster or schoolmistress on Bardsey. Naturally, Pembrokeshire refused.

Mysterious are the ways of folk memory and wisdom. There is not the slightest foundation to this belief. The historian Sir John Lloyd showed that Bardsey has been part of Caernarvonshire since that shire was first created in 1284, and we can be equally confident that it was part of the diocese of Bangor. When Deiniol, the first bishop of Bangor, died, according to a very early tradition, it was on this little island, in the midst of dangerous currents, where Cadfan, an early fellow-worker, had retired and settled in his later life, that he was buried *c*. 584.

The poet Meilyr, in the second quarter of the twelfth

century, called it '*Ynys Fair firain*' – 'the beautiful Isle of Mary'. To mediaeval people it was Ynys y Saint – Island of the Saints, and the scribe of the *Liber Landavensis*, 'The Book of Llandâf', mid twelfth century, believed twenty thousand saints had been buried there.

Chapter 2

Bardsey Island
and North-west Wales

WE KNOW NOT WHEN nor how Christianity first came to Wales. The general supposition is that it first entered Britain with the camp followers – merchants, craftsmen, officials etc. and their wives – who followed the Roman armies, as early evidence found at Caer-went (Venta Silurum) in south-east Wales, the part of Wales that was most fully Romanized, seems to confirm. It is not impossible that the Good News reached Segontium in the Caernarfon area in the time of the Romans, but as the fort was only occupied periodically the new religion had no chance to take root and spread. However, it became obvious that Wales was experiencing a great and general awakening, in nationhood and religion, in the fifth century. The two centuries from *c.* 450-650 AD are generally regarded as the golden age of the saints, the period when many of the *llannau* (early churches) were established.

Llan originally meant a plot of land. Having obtained the land, the saint would build a little church on it. In the course of time, the meaning of the word was transferred from that of the plot of land to that which was connected with it, namely the church; that is why the saint's name so often follows 'Llan'. A possible exception in the Llŷn peninsula is Llanengan. 'Engan' is the local pronunciation of 'Einion', an early king or ruler of that region, who may have given land to some unknown saint, although it is not impossible that the king himself, in old age, to atone for his sins, turned to religion and became a 'saint', i.e. that he dedicated his life completely to serving God.

It is roughly about mid fifth century that Christianity first began to penetrate into north-west Wales. But how?

In the early ages, the sea provided much traversed, popular travel routes; it was easier and safer to journey by sea than to face the dangers of vast forests and swamps on land. Archaeologists speak of the western sea-routes from the Mediterranean, with the north African coastline on one side and that of south Europe on the other, passing between the Pillars of Hercules (the Straits of Gibraltar), reaching the western peninsulas – Brittany, Cornwall, Pembroke, Llŷn, Anglesey and Ireland. The sea was a means of joining these places together, not of separating them from one another.

It was along these routes that Christians travelled from Gaul, reaching the western peninsulas. From Ireland missionaries crossed to Scotland, and penetrated inland, especially, from our point of view, to the region known as the Old North, namely southern Scotland and northern England – roughly the area between the estuaries of the Clyde and the Forth and those of the Ribble and the Humber (or Glasgow – Edinburgh in the north and Preston – Hull in the south).

From the second century BC to the seventh century AD there were periodic migrations from the Old North to north Wales.

Sometime about the middle of the fifth century, this happened on a larger scale, possibly by in *Vita*tion, in order to help the natives to drive out the Irish who had settled in parts of north Wales. Among those who came we find the families of Gildas, Einion, Deiniol, Seiriol and Maelgwn Gwynedd. It is believed that many of these families had already accepted Christianity, having been converted through the mission of Ninian, his followers and successors, from Ireland. In Llanaelhaearn church there is a memorial stone to ALIORTVS ELMETIACO, who was buried there about the year 500: Aliortus, a Christian from Elfed (Elmet), an early Brythonic kingdom corresponding roughly to the West Riding of today. Nor was he the only Christian in Llŷn; at Penprys farm, Llannor, a stone belonging to the same period, with the inscription VENDESETLI, was discovered. That would have been the contemporary form of the name Gwynhoedl, the saintly, clean-living missionary, a name that later developed into Gwnnadl, commemorated at Llangwnnadl. The stone, together with another from the same period, commemorating IOVENALIS FILI ETERNI, Iovenalis son of Edern, were removed to the Ashmolean Museum, Oxford, in 1885; they were returned in 1993, and are now at Glynyweddw, Llanbedrog.

The missionary activity of this early period was neither deliberate nor pre-arranged, rather it was a case of saints arriving, one here, one there, staying, settling, sometimes for life, sometimes for a period before moving on again. Although the sea was their highway, it could be tempestuous and dangerous, especially around rocky capes; in such circumstances, it would be wise to come ashore, carry the light craft and cross the peninsula on foot. We can imagine that is what Cybi did on his

way from Illtud's school in Morgannwg to Holyhead. He may have followed the Roman road westwards before turning to the sea. Not far from Fishguard there is a little island called Ynys Cybi. He then settled for a time in the Teifi valley, at Llangybi, then back to the sea again. Was it the stormy waves that made him come ashore in Eifionydd and establish another Llangybi? Having seen and heard of the dangerous currents around the Llŷn peninsula, he travelled across land before venturing out to sea again to reach the tiny island with its Roman fort off the west coast of Anglesey.

In the sixth century, there are signs that mission work is beginning to be planned. According to Gildas, he and, it seems, Maelgwn Gwynedd, attended Illtud's school in Morgannwg; place-names suggest Sadwrn, Tydecho, Cadfan and Deiniol had connection with the area – perhaps with the school. When Maelgwn became king of Gwynedd, Seiriol (his cousin), Cybi, Sadwrn and Deiniol were given land on which to build and every opportunity to settle. It is said that Cyngar, Mwrog, Cynfarwy, Maelog, Peulan and Llibio, whose names are connected with churches in the hundreds of Llifon and Talybolion on Anglesey, were all members of Cybi's family. We do not know whether they were actual blood relations or, more likely, members of his familia, of the religious settlement, Clas, he established within the old Roman fort on the little island later to be known as Caergybi (Cybi's Fort), in English sanctified into Holyhead

'Clas' was the usual name for the type of Celtic monastery found in Wales in the early centuries. Many of the early saints sought solitude, an isolated place, a *desertum* (Welsh *diserth*), where they could be entirely alone, devoting all their time to prayer and worship, concentrating their minds completely on God, in the hope of hearing his voice. In the early centuries, the word 'saint' implies one who devotes his life entirely to serving God. Having found such a spot, the saint would build a little church for worship and prayer and a little cell or hut in which to live. But there was something exceptionally charismatic about these people, and without realising it, they attracted others to them, individuals and families; and as everyone built a shelter for himself and family, in time there would be several huts around the little church where everyone worshipped together. That is how a clas often developed.

Briefly, a clas was a church with a community of men, women and families living a religious life under a leader or superior; Welsh priests never accepted celibacy. The head could be an abbot, as at Tywyn, a bishop, as at Bangor, and sometimes both were to be found in the same settlement, as at Llandeilo Fawr, possibly at one time. Several of the clas men would be priests, ministering not only to nearby communities but also travelling further afield, establishing new churches, returning from time to time to their teacher, their father in God at the clas; thus the original little church became the mother-church of a large area. There would also be craftsmen and labourers at the clas, to cater for the daily needs of the community.

It was on the strand – Welsh *tywyn* – between the estuaries of the rivers Dyfi and Dysynni, that Cadfan built the little church that developed into an important clas, from which he and his followers travelled considerable distances, evangelising. A century and more ago, people maintained it was possible to trace Cadfan's path from Tywyn to Llangadfan in Powys, indicating a place near Abergynolwyn where he preached, Cadfan's waterspout and Cadfan's seat. Having reached the river Dyfi, he followed it for a while and then turned south; there is a Dolgadfan near Llanbryn-mair church. Was it he who established the first church in that area, a church that was rededicated to Mair (Mary) some six centuries later? From there he crossed the high moor-land to the north-east, and established Llangadfan in the Banw valley.

His companion, Tydecho, followed the river Dyfi, establishing three churches on its bank – Cemaes, Mallwyd and Llanymawddwy near its source, from where he crossed the moor-land to the south-east to the Banw valley, building a church at Garthbeibio, some two miles west of Llangadfan. Erfyl, the patron saint of Llanerfyl, two miles south of Llangadfan, may have been a member of the same company.

Other members may have followed the Roman road from Pennal to Caersws in the Severn valley. Llonio settled at Llandinam, near the Roman fort at Caersws, but Trunio travelled down the river valley for many miles, building his church at Llandrunio, at the foot of the Breidden Mountains. Others possibly established churches closer to the clas, between the rivers Dyfi and Mawddach. Thus Tywyn gradually became the mother-church of a large area.

There is a church commemorating Sadwrn in the Tywi valley and in Anglesey. The old name for Itton in Gwent was Llanddeiniol, as if Deiniol (who may have been at Illtud's school) had started his journey eastwards before turning towards the west. There is a church bearing his name in Pembrokeshire and another in Ceredigion. At one time he evangelized in the Dee valley; there are two churches dedicated in his name in the Bala area, at Llanuwchllyn and Llanfor, then, further down the valley, at Worthenbury, Marchwiel and Bangor-on-Dee, with yet another nearer the sea at Hawarden. It was at Bangor in Arfon that he established his chief clas, and when, about the year 546, he was made bishop to oversee the spiritual welfare of Maelgwn's kingdom, it was this establishment that became the centre of the diocese.

Early in the seventh century it is possible that Beuno (d.642?), the last of the famous native saints, led a mission from Berriew near Welshpool in the Severn valley to the Dee valley and on to Clwyd as far as Llanasa and Holywell. From there he crossed to Anglesey, where he founded churches at Aberffraw and Trefdraeth. Lastly, he crossed to Arfon, establishing his chief clas at Clynnog Fawr. From Clynnog he and his followers travelled the district, evangelising and founding churches in his name at Pistyll, Carn Guwch and Botwnnog. There are more churches in north Wales dedicated in Beuno's name than in that of any other native saint. One of his disciples, Aelhaearn, followed him from the Severn valley, where he had established a church at Guilsfield; he founded another church at Llanaelhaearn near Clynnog, while his brother, Cynhaearn, settled at Ynys Cynhaearn in Eifionydd. A short distance up the Severn valley from Berriew there are two churches dedicated in the name of a third brother, Llwchaearn, at Llanllwchaearn and Llamyrewig. They were the sons of Hygarfael, lord of Llystynwynnan (Moel Feliarth), the district across the river, facing Tydecho's settlement at Garthbeibio. There were obviously families of saints.

In all probability there was a clas towards the far end of the Llŷn peninsula in the late fifth-early sixth century, its priests caring for the spiritual welfare of the surrounding countryside. Capel Anelog, Capel Cwmdyli, Capel Odo and Eglwys Cadell, of which there are no visible remains today, would all be in its care. The exact location of the clas is not known. However, two very interesting memorial stones were found on the eastern side of Anelog Mountain. About 1860, they were removed to Cefnamwlch; then, in the summer of 1992, they were taken, for their own safety, to Aberdaron church and set up on the north side of the altar, a spot in olden times reserved for the resting place of the founder of the church. One stone, in letters dated about the end of the fifth century or the beginning of the sixth, denotes the grave of a priest called VERACIVS, and the other where the priest SENACVS lay CVM MVLTITVDINEM

FRATRVM, with many brothers, making it clear this was not the cell of a lonely priest but a clas where a multitude lived together in one establishment. Study the sketch. It is not easy to read the inscription; carving letters on stone with primitive tools was difficult and tiring, and one stroke often had to serve two letters. Then think of Roman numerals. Richard White, who worked with the Gwynedd Archaeological Trust, suggested it was misreading this inscription that first gave rise to the idea that twenty thousand saints had been buried on Bardsey Island.

Senacus's memorial stone.

We do not know when the clas moved to Aberdaron. For about three centuries, from the end of the eighth century to the end of the eleventh, the area suffered severe raids at the hands of the Vikings, the pagan pirates from Scandinavia. They had managed to settle on the Scottish Islands, on the western coast of the Old North, on the Isle of Man and in Ireland, around Dublin. As many of the early saints travelled by sea important churches were often within easy reach of the sea. By this time they had collected a few treasures – vessels of precious metals, robes and cloths of expensive materials, books bound in leather and adorned with gold and gems – items that tempted these sea-rovers; they landed, plundered, burnt the building and fled. Holyhead was raided in 961, Tywyn in 963, Penmon *c.* 970, Clynnog in 978 and Bangor in 1073. In all probability, it was after these attacks came to an end that the clas was moved to Aberdaron, to a sheltered, more convenient spot. It was in a boat belonging to this religious establishment that Gruffudd ap Cynan fled to Ireland on one occasion, and it was at Aberdaron church that Rhys ap Tewdwr sought sanctuary from Gruffudd in 1115 and the country's prelates refused to hand him over to the prince of Gwynedd.

We know very little about the religious settlement on Bardsey itself in the early centuries. Even when the clasau were developing and flourishing, occasionally a saint would experience a strong desire to be alone with God. When that happened, he would retreat to a small island devoid of human habitation. According to tradition, Dyfrig spent Lent on Caldey Island, and it is believed that it was on Flatholm, in the Bristol Channel, that Gildas wrote his copy of the Gospels. The island opposite Penmon is named after St Seiriol, the two islands south-east of Abersoch are named after St Tudwal, and the little island in the Menai Straits after St Tysilio. We can imagine St Cadfan from the clas at Tywyn discovering, far away on the distant horizon, beyond the Llŷn peninsula, an ideal island to which to retreat. It is generally accepted that it was Cadfan, in the sixth century, who built the first cell on Bardsey, and that it was on Bardsey that he spent his last days on earth. The island developed into a place for retreat. It would be a convenient seclusion for the clas members of Aberdaron when they desired time for spiritual contemplation. Gradually it became a place of pilgrimage, some of the pilgrims remaining only for a time, while others desired to end their days on the island, in order to be buried in the holy ground. On the wall above the entry to the barn at Hen-dŷ, there was a stone marked with a cross of the type popular from the seventh to the ninth centuries; it has now been set in the chapel.

Somehow, sometime – how and when it is not known – a small 'regular' community, i.e. a small community of devout pious men living under a strict, specific rule, developed on the island. The earliest written reference to them is to be found in The Chronicle of the Princes, the entry concerning the death of Iarddur, a monk from Bardsey, in 1011. Why he should deserve an entry in the Chronicle we are not told. The remaining part of another carved memorial stone on the island belongs to the end of the tenth century, or the beginning of the eleventh, according to the experts.

Writing an account of his journey through Wales during Lent 1188, Giraldus Cambrensis noted, 'There lies beyond Llŷn a small island where very religiously strict monks live, called

The Bardsey Cross.

Coelibes (unmarried men) or *Colidei* (worshippers of God).' These were the Culdees, members of an old monastic order found in Ireland and in Scotland, where they had monasteries from the ninth to the thirteenth century. The name derived from the Irish *célé Dé*, meaning 'servant of God'. They were hermits, living together in poverty, celibacy and obedience, in the strict self-disciplined tradition of St Illtud, his followers and the early saints. They had a settlement too at Beddgelert. About the year 1200, the community adopted the Rule of St Augustine, a rule that observed similar ideals, and joined the Order of Augustinian Canons. The community at Beddgelert adopted the same rule, and later a small community settled on the eastern St Tudwal Island.

It was after joining the Order of Augustinian Canons that St Mary's Abbey on Bardsey was founded; the earliest remains belong to the thirteenth century.

Although it was the policy of the Norman invaders to abolish the native clasau, the Aberdaron clas suffered little interference, possibly because of its remoteness and insignificance. However, many of its lands were transferred to the new abbey on Bardsey, mainly in the township of Uwch Sely at the far end of the peninsula, that of Is Sely, between the rivers Saint and Daron, Ultradaron is a long strip along the coast from Aberdaron to a point a little further than Llawenan, and Tremorfa, roughly the present day parishes of Bryncroes and Llangwnnadl. The situation is complicated by the fact that some holdings remained in the hands of members of the clas.

After the dissolution, *c.* 1537, the government made a survey of the abbey; there was nothing on the island apart from the abbey buildings, and they were all empty. Today all that remains is the tower within a recent cemetery.

.

Chapter 3

To Undertake a Pilgrimage – Whither?

*T*HE NEW CATHOLIC ENCYCLOPAEDIA defines pilgrimage as 'a journey (usually of considerable duration) made to some sacred place, as an act of religious devotion', and *The Oxford English Dictionary* as 'a journey to a sacred shrine or sanctuary for a religious motive', adding that from this developed the idea of our life on earth as a journey to a blessed resting place later on.

A journey made to a sacred place, to shrines or sepulchres, as an act of religious devotion. Primitive people believed that the gods had chosen some sites on earth in which to dwell, and carried thither the produce of the land, crops and animals, as offerings to deities. If we turn to the Old Testament we find that the Israelites were expected, according to the Law, to keep three Pilgrim Feasts, and journeyed to Jerusalem to celebrate the Feast of the Unleavened Bread (Easter), the Pentecost and the Feast of the Tabernacles. It is possible that these feasts originally served an agricultural purpose, of asking God's blessing on the land and its crops and giving thanks for the harvest, but that gradually they developed historical symbolism, commemorating being led from the Egyptian house of bondage, receiving the Law, and their journey in the wilderness. Psalms 120-134 are the jubilant songs that they used to sing as they ascended towards Jerusalem for the Feast of the Tabernacles.

Christians regarded life as a pilgrimage. According to St Augustine there is no rest for the soul except with God. Seeking God, in different places and through different works, is what is meant by pilgrimage. Undertaking a devotional journey in this world was a means to this end.

Very early – possibly before the end of the first century AD – pilgrims would visit places made holy by the life of Christ, where events recounted in the New Testament had occurred. By the fourth century the emperor Constantine and his followers had built churches in some of the most important locations, and pilgrims could behold, through the eyes of faith, the events mentioned in the Scriptures and try to realise the life of Christ. To visit this Holy Land was the pilgrim's predominant desire throughout the centuries.

Early in the Christian era, martyrs were regarded as men and women who had deservedly won eternal life. Did not Stephen, the first martyr for the Christian faith, testify, "Behold I see the heavens opened, and the Son of man standing at the right hand of God" (Acts, 7.56)? People came to believe that complete forgiveness of sins could be obtained by praying and meditating at a martyr's grave, and by the second century, Rome, where the martyrs Peter and Paul were buried, had become a popular place to visit. Rome was the most important religious centre of Western Europe throughout the Middle Ages.

A rifai greiriau Rufain
A rifai'r môr, ef, a'r main,
Gwyrthiau heb ei gywerthydd
Gan un o'r rhain a'm gwnai'n rhydd.

[He who could count the relics of Rome could count the sea and the stones, miracles by one of these unequalled objects would make me free.] Thus said the poet Huw Cae Llwyd, who went there on a pilgrimage, together with his son Ieuan, in 1475. 'To be made free': 'a free soul' was the term used to describe the condition of one who had received from the Church official forgiveness and absolution from sin.

No one can deny that the Holy Land and Rome are genuinely linked to the history of Christianity. Unfortunately, some centres became popular on account of unfounded legends. In the ninth century, the grave of the apostle James was 'discovered' at Galicia in north-west Spain and St Iago de Compostela developed into an important centre. While demolishing a church in Milan, *c.* 1158, the graves of the wise men, the magi were 'found'; in 1164 their bodies were moved to Cologne, and the Three Kings of Cologne began to be honoured.

By the third century AD, men and women who had devoted their whole life to serving God, striving to attain perfection, people full of God's power and sanctity, came to be regarded as saints, and it was believed that they, too, when departing from this earthly life, were accepted directly into God's presence, to become citizens of the heavenly Jerusalem, the community of saints. According to the teaching of the Church, these people, through their worthiness and prayers, could defend their fellow Christians on earth, and it was lawful for humans to pray for their help; although they themselves had no personal power. God occasionally granted them the power to perform miracles in this world. In mediaeval times, these ideas greatly appealed to ordinary people. Local saints were men and women who had trodden this part of the earth; everyone was well acquainted with them, having heard them mentioned in sermons, and their *Vitae* read in church on their feast days. It was so much easier to pray to these local saints – our own dear little saints, as Sir Ifor Williams called them – than to the invisible God whom no one had ever seen. They were very acceptable mediators between God and mankind.

Since the saints were regarded as mediators, so too were pilgrimages to places connected with them regarded as a means of obtaining forgiveness for sins; should a miracle have occurred there, the appeal would be even greater. That is how St Winefred's well at Holywell achieved such prominence. According to the story contained in Beuno's *Vita*, one day when Winefred's parents were in Beuno's church, attending mass, king Caradog came to their house and tried to have their daughter as a concubine. She managed to escape but the king followed her; he caught her by the door of the church, drew his sword and cut off her head. Beuno and Winefred's parents came out of the church, and Beuno berated the king, "I beseech God not to save thee and not to respect thee any more than didst thou respect this maiden." The king dissolved into a pool of water and was never seen again on this earth. Then, Beuno placed the maiden's head back on her body, spread his mantle over her, and he and her parents returned into the church to continue with the mass. When they came out, Winefred arose completely healed. Where her blood had fallen on the ground a well gushed forth and that well to this day heals men and beasts of their afflictions.

As mentioned (p.30), several saints retreated from time to time to a little island devoid of human habitation, in order to have peace to pray, meditate and to listen for the voice of God. Naturally, an island connected with a saint or saints would have a special attraction, and it was believed that to die there and be buried close to the servants of God was an undeniable aid for all Christians to join the happy band of saints. There is no reason to doubt the tradition that Deiniol was buried on Bardsey, he and possibly many other saints. In the course of the centuries Bardsey became a resort for pilgrims, and a special place to which to retreat to prepare for the world to come. To be buried there was what many desired, those in holy orders and lay people; as the poet Meilyr expressed in his 'Marwysgafn', his death-bed poem, sometime during the second quarter of the twelfth century:

> Creawdr a'm crewys a'm cynnwys i
> Ymhlith plwyf gwirin gwerin Enlli.

[May the Creator who created me include me among the holy inhabitants of Bardsey.] The scribe who wrote the *Liber Landavensis*, The Book of Llandâf, about the middle of the twelfth century, refers to the island as the Rome of Britain, on account of the long, dangerous journey to the furthermost extreme of the kingdom, and on account of its sanctity and purity with twenty thousand saints buried there. Giraldus Cambrensis did not state the number; 'Here, according to tradition, the bodies of numerous saints have been buried,' was his remark, when he travelled through Wales with Archbishop Baldwin of Canterbury during Lent 1188.

Chapter 4

To Undertake a Pilgrimage –
Why and How?

T HERE MUST HAVE BEEN some exceptionally strong
inducement, some great stimulus to cause men and
women to leave their locality and undertake a pilgrimage to
the remotest places, facing dangers and hardships of which we
today are totally unaware. There were neither eating places nor
shops available, not to mention guest houses and taverns, and
no public transport of any kind, except when crossing a sea or a
wide river. A journey to Rome or Jerusalem would take many,
many months if not years, and the journey to St David's was so
difficult and dangerous that Pope Callixtus II, *c.* 1120, decreed
that to go to St David's twice was equivalent to one journey to
Rome, and to go there three times equivalent to one journey
to Jerusalem. It was also believed that to go to Bardsey three
times was equivalent to one journey to Rome. As stated (p.38)
the scribe who wrote the Book of Llandaf refers to Bardsey as
the Rome of Britain, on account of the long and dangerous
journey and of its sanctity and purity.

Despite all the dangers, hundreds of people went on
pilgrimages, with clerics from Wales and Ireland among those
most diligently devotional. By the twelfth century the pilgrims

who visited Rome and Jerusalem were so numerous that their numbers had to be restricted. (Was that one reason why St David's and Bardsey were thus honoured?)

Why undertake such hard labour and encounter such perils? There were several reasons: some went with wholehearted resolve; others were compelled to go; and as with any movement and custom, there were followers, together with professional profiteers. Men and women whose sincere minds simply sought salvation for their souls were the most genuine and devotional pilgrims. They were not guilty of any visible misdeed, but, feeling guilt in their hearts, had to be rid of it before they could be reconciled with God. They were seeking God, trying to discern him in different localities and through various deeds, always concentrating their whole attention on God.

Entreating and thanksgiving, again, were strong factors. Saints were regarded as mediators, mediators who could beg for supernatural help towards healing soul and body. It was possible at a saint's tomb to ask for help in adversity, e.g. to free someone from prison in this country or in a foreign land, to be delivered from famine and pestilence, and especially for the healing of wounds and sickness – possibly the most obvious request. When one considers how much of his time Christ devoted to healing the sick during his sojourn on earth, it is not surprising that people, when the medical profession was almost entirely worthless, turned to saints and longed for miracles.

Some people, when they faced a crisis or trouble, vowed they would go on a pilgrimage. Others undertook the journey to give thanks for a deliverance, or for a victory over an enemy, and a few simply to give thanks for the blessings they had received in this life.

Occasionally a pilgrimage was imposed as a penance for misdeeds. Murderers and the worst miscreants were sent on a pilgrimage that would last for many years. Thus society would be rid of them; it was a means of banishing criminals.

It was possible to undertake a pilgrimage on behalf of someone else, at that person's expense, while he was still alive and able; and just as money was left in wills to pay a priest to say mass for the soul, so, too, occasionally, money was left to enable someone to undertake a pilgrimage for the bequeather's soul. This could give rise to an almost professional type of pilgrim.

Then there were the followers, the hangers-on. Some joined for the interest and joy of seeing holy places, some just to see a little more of the world. Naturally, going on a pilgrimage was a chance to escape from the monotony of everyday life, and was a respectable and lawful excuse, in the eyes of the world and of the church, to avoid work.

Before leaving his circle and surroundings, abandoning at least for a time his old life, the pilgrim was advised to put everything in order. He was to return any money he had obtained by illegal means; if he owned any lands he had to arrange who was to look after them, and every pilgrim had to arrange support and care for his family while he would be away, bearing in mind that possibly he would not return. He was asked to give alms, that being the surest way of securing a place in heaven for his soul whatever happened. He would be well advised to obtain a letter from his bishop, affirming that he was a genuine pilgrim; the letter would safeguard him from being accused of being a robber or a wayfarer who took advantage of others.

The last act he performed before setting off on his travels was to go to church to hear mass, and receive a special blessing.

Notice the little carving in the church of Llangynin, west of Carmarthen. The pilgrim's dress was plain and unadorned, as befitted a penitent.. He wore a low-crowned hat with a wide brim, carried a wallet or scrip on his back, and in his hand the pilgrim's long staff tipped with iron.

Well to-do people travelled on horseback; there were special places at intervals on the road from London to Canterbury, and on to the continent, where horses could be changed. The majority, however, walked, but not often alone; for safety's sake, to have company and to support one another, physically and spiritually, there was a tendency for small groups to journey together.

The chosen route was not always the shortest and most direct; a long, difficult journey added to the penance and that would help to obtain absolution. Churches and sepulchres were visited on the way, and the sick and the wounded would be given opportunity to partake of the healing powers of relics

The Llangynin Carving.

and wells. They endured extreme hardships, what with severe weather, thieves, wild animals (there were wolves even in Wales in those days), and often hunger and the lack of shelter. In foreign countries they had to be on their guard against infidels, especially the Saracens in Spain and Palestine. In many places the only means of obtaining food was by begging; fortunately, alms giving was regarded the greatest virtue of all by the church. Naturally, there would be a room allocated to pilgrims in a monastery, where they could obtain food, a bed, rest, care and comfort, but there were long distances where there was neither monastery nor friary nor a hospice. In some places a lodging-house was built especially for pilgrims. At such places there could be pilgrims from other regions or countries and there would be much talking, exchanging news and sagas. On such an occasion a follower, especially the professional pilgrim, got his chance to entertain the company by relating the wonders he had seen and the adventures that had befallen him, giving free rein to his imagination.

It is quite possible that many mediaeval sagas grew and developed in such circumstances. It is generally accepted that there is an obvious connection between the Charlemagne legends and the pilgrim route through the Roncevalles pass to Saint Iago in north-west Spain. Travellers called at churches, would be told the stories by the monks, and as every church tried to surpass the others stories grew and developed. Should there be followers or professional pilgrims in the group it would be very easy for a story to travel from one country to another, possibly allocating to it a new locality in their own country, developing a local legend into an international popular tale. In much the same way, resting on a pilgrimage to Bardsey could provide an opportunity to listen to many local stories, possibly adding to one occasionally. Unfortunately, only a small portion of our early tales have survived; brief references in the Stanzas of the Graves and the Triads prove how very much richer our saga tradition was at one time. We gather from those that have survived, in particular the Four Branches of the Mabinogi, that they were transmitted orally; they were composed not to be read but to be told, and that by a professional storyteller. Naturally, wonders and supernatural events were what appealed most; but one cannot help noticing the local detail, especially in the two branches of the Mabinogi dealing with north Wales, Branwen daughter of Llyr and Math son of Mathonwy.

Having arrived at his destination, the pilgrim had to complete his penance. He would kneel for a long time on the hard floor or bare earth to pray, often throughout the night. Sometimes he would wear sackcloth and lie on ashes, eating and drinking only the bare minimum necessary to keep him alive. Perhaps he would have to walk around a grave or sanctuary a set number of times, lighting candles and burning incense. He was expected to bring an offering with him: animals, gems and precious metals, models in wax or metal of limbs that had been healed, or a tablet recording the escape granted to him. Having done all that was required of him, there would be a priest at hand to hear his confession, then, having confessed, he would receive the sacrament. His sins would now have been forgiven, but before he could obtain full remission, and enjoy all the privileges of reconciliation with God, he had to perform an act of penance; he had to renounce self completely and work for others, for all who needed help, e.g. fast, pray for others, devote himself to good works and give alms. Not until he had completed all this would he receive complete absolution, and enjoy a free soul.

With their souls at peace, the pilgrims were in no hurry to return. Some remained there for a long time, ministering to the sick and helping the priests' servants with their work. A few would decide to remain there for the rest of their lives in the hope that they too would be buried in the sacred place, among a great crowd of witnesses, and be counted among the happy company of saints. But these pilgrims were in a minority; sooner or later, most would begin the long journey back to their homes.

Pilgrims could hardly return empty-handed, they had to have some visible token, not only to prove that they had been to the sacred place but because they believed that the spirit of the place would be in the article and that the article would be an aid for those who had not had the opportunity to partake of such blessings. A relic was the greatest token of all: part, however small, of a saint or a martyr, or something associated with Christ, such as a piece of the Cross. Failing this, one had to be content with a representative relic, an object that had been in contact with the body or grave of a saint. Small metal objects were sold, such as a ring, a brooch, or vessels that were said to have touched a holy person. It was possible to buy small phials containing water from the river Jordan or a healing well, oil from the sanctuary lamps, and, in Palestine, phials containing the milk of the Virgin Mary's breast. Back home, these could be placed on the sick or the injured for easement and cure. Even a few stones or a handful of dust from a sacred place were believed to be full of virtue.

Badges were also sold. Look at the sketch of the carving in Llandyfodwg church, Morgannwg. This suggests a professional pilgrim; he looks neither weak nor miserable. This is no poor traveller, his is no ordinary scrip but one adorned with three tassels. Probably the staff over his left shoulder at one time had palm leaves, a sign that he had been to Jericho. The crosses prove he had been to Christ's sepulchre, and the cross keys to St Peter's grave in Rome. (Had he visited both places twice?) It was at St Iago in Spain that he got the shell. Another sign that could be bought in Rome was

The Llandyfodwg Carving.

a copy of the Vernacle, a cloth with Christ's face imposed on it: when Veronica used her napkin to wipe the sweat from Christ's face, on his way to the cross, the image of his face remained on it. The head of John the Baptist was displayed on the Amiens badges. We can imagine the professional pilgrim collecting all these and making a great display of them.

Undertaking pilgrimages became an established part of Christian devotion, especially from the eleventh century to the fifteenth century; but although it was recommended by the Church and proved to be a spiritual aid to many, it was not regarded as 'necessary to salvation'. Be that as it may; the custom had obvious merits. It did one good to shake oneself free of the rut of apathy; travelling to new areas and meeting different people was good therapy, and the opportunity to see and discuss widened one's horizons. If he gained peace for his soul then the pilgrim was much happier and a better man for his community.

Chapter 5

To the Far End of Llŷn – From the North

Bangor

Pentir

Segontium   afon Seiont

Llanbeblig

Dinas
Dinlle

Llanwnda

Llandwrog

Clynnog Fawr

Nant
Gwrtheyrn

Llanaelhaearn

Beddgelert

Pistyll

Nefyn

Llangwnnadl

Bodferin

Uwch
Mynydd

Mynydd Anelog

Aberdaron

Harlech

Ynys Enlli

BEFORE WE START ON our journey, it would be as well to explain what the word 'road' implied in the Middle Ages. We know the Romans were experts at building paved roads and for a few centuries after they left these remained in fairly good condition and were an asset as well as a convenience to both travellers and trade. Such a road existed from Caerhun in the Conwy valley to Segontium (Caer-saint), the fort on the river Saint or Seiont, the Roman fort in Arfon. A similar road ran from Segontium to Bryncir, to Tomen-y-mur in the parish of Maentwrog, and on to Pennal, a short distance east of Tywyn; but there were no Roman roads leading westwards from Segontium, there was no such road to Llŷn. West of Segontium we have to forget about a clearway of a certain width with a hard surface and definite edges. Very often road meant no more than a legal right, through custom and usage, to travel over the land from one village to another; it would have no distinct sides but much tramping over long periods would have hardened the surface here and there, giving in places a sense of direction. In other places, one could only aim for some visible landmark or other – a tree, a rock or a building – as we today, when crossing moor-land, aim for a lone tree, thorn bushes or a pointed crag. Early churches did not have spires and towers, but they were bigger and better buildings than ordinary dwellings, and there were many churches on the way to Llŷn.

Having attended mass at St Deiniol's church, Bangor, and received the special blessing for pilgrims, the traveller was ready to start on his journey. The valley of the river Adda could be marshy, and it is quite possible he would follow the Maes Glas (Green Field) path up Bangor Mountain, the way the monks went from the clas to the church at Pentir. The Roman road to Segontium would pass somewhere not far from Pentir and could be followed to Llanbeblig church, close to that fort. There had been a village in that area from early times; then, about 1090, the Earl of Chester built a mound and castle near the estuary of the river Seiont, but by 1115 the native Welsh had regained the site and developed a small centre. In pre-Norman times the place was sometimes referred to as Hen Gaer Cystennin (Constantine's Old Fort), and Capel Helen (Helen's Chapel) stood close by.

Trying to discover how these names derived is a most interesting exercise. In the course of generations and centuries many stories and traditions developed around Segontium. Mention was made earlier (p.22) how, about the middle of the fifth century, tribes from the Old North settled in north Wales. Their ancestors would have been familiar with Magnus Maximus, Macsen Wledig (Macsen the Ruler) as the Welsh people called him, head of the Roman army in Britain, who made special arrangements with the inhabitants of one of the native provinces of the Old North, the Gododdin, before crossing to the continent in 383 AD, to claim the title Emperor of Rome. His wife was Elen, daughter of Eudaf, the Brythonic chieftain who ruled Segontium.

In the early centuries there was a stone at Segontium with the name CONSTANTINUS inscribed on it, not an uncommon name among the Romans; the Welsh form of the name would be Cystennin. Nennius, a disciple of bishop Elfoddw of Gwynedd, writing about the year 800, knew of this stone, and stated that it was the tombstone of Constantinus, son of the first Christian Roman Emperor, Constantine the Great (307-337), who had come to Britain and died here. Since the name of Constantine the Great's mother was Helena it was very easy to identify her with Elen, daughter of Eudaf from Segontium. Tradition maintained that Helena, mother of

Constantine, had discovered the true cross of Christ, thus, on the strength of this, Elen daughter of Eudaf became a saint and a chapel near Segontium was attributed to her. By the fourteenth century, a resplendent Welsh saga, 'The Dream of Macsen', had developed, relating how Macsen Wledig, Emperor of Rome, having seen in a dream the most beautiful maiden in the whole world, journeyed to the Fort in Arfon to seek Elen for his bride. As legends develop the correct order of generations and eras are ignored and characters and events are combined. It would be interesting to know what the pilgrims contributed to the story.

After 1282 the king of England, Edward I, built a strong castle close by, and established a borough enclosed with turreted walls. He and his assistants were aware of these stories; the walls of Caernarfon and its castle were built on the pattern of those of Constantinople, as the men who had been on a crusade were well aware. The natives were removed from the new town and replaced by foreigners. For a time Caernarfon was a town to be avoided and by-passed.

By the fifteenth century, however, the town had an effigy that attracted pilgrims, 'Jesus of Caernarfon', a figure of

Iesu grys dyfrwaed ar groes dirion

[Jesus with his shirt soaked with blood and water on a fair cross] nailed to the cross with three nails, i.e. his feet were crossed so that one nail went through both feet, increasing the pain and suffering. In a poem to the effigy, the priest-poet, Sir Gruffudd Fain ap Llywelyn, stressed the deep wounds and pain, because it was through these that forgiveness and blessedness were obtained, and it is by trying to endure these in our own bodies that we will obtain deliverance. On the Day of Judgment, when Christ appears on the rainbow in all his wounds and passion, the poet pleads,

> Cadw ni 'nghyd i'th fryd er dy fron, ferthyr,
> A Thŵr yr Eryr a thre'r goron.

[Keep us and the Eagle Tower and the crown borough together in thy mind for your heart's sake, martyr.] 'Jesus' Fort' was what the poet called the town.

After leaving Llanbeblig it was necessary to find a convenient place to cross the river Seiont in order to aim for Llanfaglan and its well. The large stone, with a cross carved on it sometime between the seventh and ninth centuries, known as 'Maen Beuno', now in Clynnog church, is thought to have been somewhere in this region originally. According to tradition, it was at one time by Glan Beuno, then near Bodwyn, before being taken to Aberglaslyn Hall; it was moved to Clynnog church in 1919. Could it have been some kind of pointer for pilgrims aiming for Beuno's church at Clynnog? With the sea on the right one was not likely to go astray, but it was essential to know where to cross marshy ground and small estuaries safely.

Proceeding towards Llanwnda and Llandwrog, one takes a rest at Edliw's Well. Before long travellers will see Dinas Dinlle(u) (Lleu's Fort), and out in the sea Caer Aranrhod (Aranrhod's Fort) and Trwyn Maen Dylan (the Promontory Dylan's Rock). These provide an excuse to tell of the adventures of Math, Gwydion and Gilfaethwy, who lived in the area when the world was very young; how they managed to deceive Pryderi, lord of Dyfed, and bring home to Gwynedd some of the new animals, pigs, that Pwyll, Pryderi's father, had received as a gift from the king of the other world. It would also be a chance to tell the story of Aranrhod and her son, Dylan, who could swim as well as the best fish in the sea; and of the other son, who his mother swore would never be given either a name or arms or a wife, and how Gwydion, by magic and charm, managed to get the mother herself to name him Lleu, to put on his armour for him, and for a wife, Math and Gwydion conjured from the flowers of the field the fairest maiden ever seen and called her Blodeuwedd (i.e. the face of flowers).

In all probability, Clynnog Fawr would be the most important stop on the way since St Beuno's church itself was a well known centre of pilgrimages. It was essential to spend some time here.

In pilgrim times the church would be very small, even smaller than the present Beuno Chapel; the large church of today dates from about 1480-1520, the chapel being rebuilt, on a larger scale, about the same time. But there would have been other buildings close by, as one would expect in a clas; old foundations have been discovered, but not on a sufficient scale to suggest what buildings they were. In the days of the clas there would have been accommodation here for pilgrims and travellers.

In the course of the centuries many stories have been recounted about St Beuno: about the numerous miracles he performed, how he resurrected several people from the dead, among them Gwenfrewy (St Winefred), whose healing well at Holywell was a popular centre for pilgrims (p.37). By the fourteenth century, Beuno's *Vita* was well known, and considered of sufficient merit and importance for the Anchorite of Llanddewibrefi to include it, with that of St David, in the collection of religious texts he compiled for Gruffudd ap Llywelyn ap Phylip ap Trahaearn of Cantref Mawr in 1346. The *Vita* declares that Beuno, when dying, saw the heavens opening and heard the voice of God calling him. Early in the fifteenth century Rhys Goch Eryri, the poet from Beddgelert, versified an account in an eulogy. The seventh day before Easter, Beuno, on his sick bed, saw the gates of heaven and the whole firmament open, and the martyrs and archangels

> Yn dwyn pob glân wasanaeth
> Ar gôr main i'r Gŵr a'u maeth

[bringing every holy service in a tuneful choir to the One who nurtured them]. Present were Dewi and Deiniol, Peter and Paul, and all the company of heaven, 'And Mary, a sun among them'. Since he had lived on water and barley bread, Beuno heard

> Wiw Dduw yn ei wahodd ef

[the true God inviting him] to the eternal feast of the heavenly kingdom

> Gyda'r Tad yn y gadair
> A'r Mab a'r Ysbryd a Mair.

[With the Father in the chair, and the Son and the Spirit and Mary.] The *Vita* would be read in the church on the saint's feast day, and special prayers would also be offered.

Outside the church there is a flat pillar, about six feet six inches high, and on the face of the pillar (not on top of it) a very significant sundial, a type that was common in Ireland from the tenth to the twelfth centuries but, until very recently, when a similar one was discovered at Tywyn, was the only one known in Wales. Close to the top of the pillar there is a style-hole for a gnomon bar (the projecting piece that shows the time by its shadow), and beneath it a semi-circle divided into four equal segments, denoting the four divisions for the Hours and Services of the clas. We can imagine how pilgrims would stare with amazement at the sundial.

At these set hours the clas members left their work and prayed. The Psalms played an important part in the early worship, only a small number of the clas members could read, but they could all learn the Psalms by heart, and the pilgrims would have the opportunity to join them. Did they intone, and that in more than one voice? According to Giraldus Cambrensis, the Welsh people sang in many voices and in many modes and keys, and had become perfect not through skill but through the practice of ages. At a clas as important as Clynnog one would expect singing in harmony.

St Beuno's well is to be found some two hundred yards

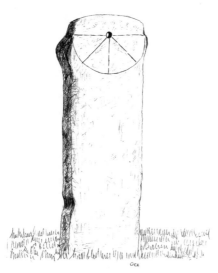

The Clynnog Sundial.

in the direction of Llanaelhaearn. It was the custom to immerse the sick persons in the well, and then put them to lie over night on a bed of rushes on Beuno's grave in the chapel.

There are several Christian symbols at Llanaelhaearn: memorial stones to Aliortus and Melitus, dating from *c.* 500, and a stone marked with a cross from the period seventh to the ninth centuries. Travellers waited by St Aelhaearn's well for the stirring of the waters;

The Llanaelhaearn Cross.

when bubbles suddenly appeared from the bottom of the well that was the time to step into it.

Now came the most strenuous part of the journey: they had to climb the slope of Yr Eifl Mountain (The Rivals), then through the gap and down to Nefyn.

A lodging-house for pilgrims had been built above Nant Gwrtheyrn. It would be interesting to know what stories were told about king Gwrtheyrn. Should there be in the company a monk or traveller who had stayed at Beddgelert priory, it is more than likely that they would hear how Gwrtheyrn fled to the strongest place in his kingdom, to the mountain a little to the east of Beddgelert. There the wonder child, Emrys, born without a father, explained to him why he could not build a fort there, and interpreted the significance of the fight between the white dragon and the red dragon. When he realized that he could not stay there, as he had intended, Gwrtheyrn gave the place to the infant prodigy, and ever since it has been known by his name, Dinas Emrys. The story of St Garmon is tied up with that of Gwrtheyrn; and with a Llanarmon in Eifionydd, most likely they would hear of his doings as well. These stories were regarded as ancient when Nennius recorded them about the year 800.

On again, along the shore to Pistyll farmhouse, a homestead that was freed from paying tithe to the church on condition that it welcomed pilgrims.

Of all the churches on the journey today the one at Pistyll resembles most a church of the time of the pilgrims. It is possible that two thirds of it, the western end, belong to the twelfth century, the eastern third being added in the fifteenth century. Unfortunately, the remains of a mural on the north wall of the chancel have deteriorated too much to be deciphered. It has been suggested that it was a picture of St Christopher, the patron saint of travellers, but one would expect to find his effigy opposite the door, so that travellers

The Pistyll Font.

could open the door, look in, kneel, offer a short prayer, and continue on their journey. Could it have been a picture of St Beuno, the founder of the church? And was that why it was wrongly believed that he had been buried under the altar?

We know of four stones marked with a cross, indicating the way for pilgrims, between Pistyll and Nefyn. The first was originally in a field in the parish of Pistyll; later, in order to make work easier for the farmer, it was set on top of a wall by Tir-bach, on the side of the present road leading to Nefyn. The second was on the boundary of the parishes of Pistyll and Nefyn; this was removed to form the door lintel to a cowshed. The third was on an ancient grave mound, and since it got the name 'Carreg y Bwgan' (bogey/ghost stone) it was deliberately destroyed. The fourth was near the present vicarage, by the road leading to the beach. Like the Llanaelhaearn stone, they

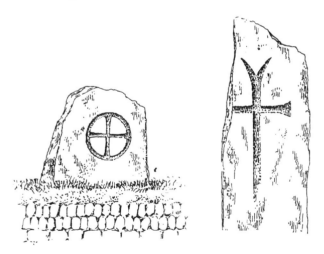

The Pistyll Cross (left) and the Nefyn Cross.

belong to the period from the seventh to the ninth centuries.

From the end of the twelfth century onwards Nefyn was developing into the administrative centre of the commot of Dinllaen and its trade increasing. It was not simply a herring market only; a variety of goods was available for those with money, including small objects made by local goldsmiths that could be presented as an offering on Bardsey. There was also a small priory here. Although Nefyn was a borough, it was not walled, and its inhabitants were native Welsh. Pilgrims were an important link between them and the wide world beyond Yr Eifl. They listened attentively, gaping wide most likely, to what the visitors had to say about places that were so different from their own small circle, and to the news they brought, though it must have been far from new by then. With such appreciative listeners the speakers' memories would expand more and more. Nefyn was a bigger and busier town than Pwllheli, until it was devastated during the Glyndŵr rebellion.

On again, with the sea on the right. Where exactly would Edern church be in those days? We know little more than their names about many of the saints of Llŷn; there must surely be others, 'who have no memorial'. It is possible, however, that memory of some still survived in the early centuries of the Middle Ages and that the local priests recounted to the pilgrims the signs and favour that God had shown them and the miracles they had performed. We still have the Christian memorial stones from the early sixth century: VENDESETLI (Gwynhoedl >Gwnnadl) found near Beudy'r Mynydd, Penprys; FIGULINUS son of LOCULITUS from Llannor, and IOVENALIS son of Edern; folk memory and wisdom could easily have kept alive and developed tales about them. Close to every church there was a well, endowed with numerous stories about the lame walking, the deaf hearing, the dumb speaking, the blind seeing and the sick healed. We can be certain advantage was taken of every opportunity for healing (and when we remember how rarely they washed in those days, immersion could not fail to make them feel more comfortable).

Only the centre part of Llangwnnadl church would have been in existence in the days of the pilgrims; the two side aisles were added in the sixteenth century. Would the old Celtic hand-bell have been there in those days? According to local tradition, it was discovered under the hearth at Bryn-y-gloch,

The Llangwnnadl Bell.

Penllech. This hand-bell, oblong not round, with a serpent's head carved at both ends of the handle, belongs to the tenth century. Similar bells were to be found in Ireland from the ninth to the eleventh centuries. The Order of Culdees was connected with Ireland and Bardsey. The original bell is now at the National Museum in Cardiff, with a replica at Llangwnnadl. In the church there is also a stone with a cross that could date from *c.* 600.

In pilgrimage times there was also a church or chapel at Bodferin; the remains are visible today.

Anelog Mountain will now be in sight. The original clas was somewhere on its slopes in the early centuries, before being moved to Aberdaron. Having arrived at this area there would be a chance to rest, and to visit the small chapels of the district, to pray and present offerings before facing the dangers of the stormy Bardsey Sound.

Chapter 6

To the Far End of Llŷn – From the South

I T WAS CADFAN, THE founder of the clas at Tywyn, Merioneth, who built the first little cell on Bardsey, about the same time as Deiniol was establishing the clas at Bangor. From Tywyn, as stated (p.26), Cadfan and his followers diligently preached the gospel, often penetrating far inland, so that Tywyn, gradually, became the mother-church of the commot of Ystumanner and the centre of pilgrimages.

Although so little is known about the native clasau, it is not unreasonable to suppose that learning was well to the fore at

Tywyn Church.

Tywyn in the twelfth century. Travelling by sea, it was within easy reach of Llanbadarn Fawr, a clas famous for its learning in the eleventh and twelfth centuries, in the days of Bishop Sulien, Sulien the Wise, and his talented sons and grandsons. His son Rhigyfarch was the author of St David's *Vita*; he and his brother Ieuan composed Latin verse, and extremely fine illuminated capitals formed by Ieuan adorn manuscripts. One Welsh *englyn*, extolling Cyrwen, Padarn's crosier, exists in Ieuan's handwriting; whether he or someone else was the author, it is obvious that Ieuan was interested in the Welsh bardic tradition. These men were well versed in the classics, and also well acquainted with Welsh and Irish sagas – Sulien had spent ten years in Ireland at a time when committing native sagas to writing enjoyed prominence in the monasteries. It would be quite natural for some of this learning to penetrate to Tywyn.

When Gruffudd ap Cynan, after a long struggle, repossessed the kingdom of Gwynedd, early in the twelfth century, establishing more peace than had been enjoyed for a long time, the people of Gwynedd laboured to cultivate the land, and to build and renew churches. Several of the principal churches were built on a Norman plan popular at the time for important churches: a church on the pattern of a cross with fairly short transepts and an aisle-less nave. Although Tywyn church has been restored from time to time, the plan is still visible, and parts of the structure date from the twelfth century.

When the poet Llywelyn visited Tywyn, mid twelfth century, he found a magnificent church. The new church would be much bigger than the earlier churches: Tywyn church was

'Uchel-lan Gadfan ger glan glas fôr'

[the high church of Cadfan by the shore of the blue sea] with its lime-washed walls gleaming in the sun. 'Fel eglwys Dewi y'i digoned', it had been built and furnished as richly as St David's. It had three altars: one to Mary – it was the period when the cult of the Virgin was beginning to spread in Wales; an altar to St Peter – Peter was connected with warfare, and did not the name Cadfan imply a skilful man in battle? (*Cad*) 'defender of warriors' was what the poet Llywelyn called him; the third altar, namely the high altar, that came as a gift from heaven, was to St Cadfan. The saint's crosier was a defence against enemies as it made them turn and fight one another. It was 'a church of faith and religion, belief and communion', with many priests, and its choir merited praise. Ordinary, poor, workaday folk would be totally amazed to see such a church; its ceremonies and processions, its resplendent robes and singing would bring colour and richness to their austere, monotonous lives.

In the clas, in the company of the abbot Morfran, feasts with mead and abundance of good food were enjoyed, with the generous abbot presenting the poet with horses. The members composed poetry, and the poet Llywelyn enjoyed their discussion. The clas at Tywyn was one of the most important in north Wales.

Somewhere in the area there was an exceptional memorial stone, dating from the eighth century, a stone with the inscription in Welsh, not in Latin, as was usual at that time. In the days of the pilgrims, the letters would be clear and the wording definite. Was there a sad story about the three who were buried first, then the fourth later on? The stone, with the inscription very badly weathered and worn, is to be seen today in Tywyn church.

Pilgrims from the south would most likely stay for a while at Tywyn before resuming their long journey to the island on the far distant horizon. A pilgrimage was not to be rushed; it was a journey to be undertaken leisurely, over a long period.

Having decided to proceed, pilgrims had the choice of either keeping to the coast or following the old Roman roads.

Following the coast had its advantages: for the first part of the journey they would be able to see Bardsey, and there were several churches to act as guiding landmarks; on the other hand, there were treacherous and marshy estuaries to be crossed. Giraldus Cambrensis and Archbishop Baldwin crossed several estuaries by boat in 1188, but the archbishop could demand service and he had money to pay; not so the poor pilgrims.

First of all, we shall follow the coast, going past St Cadfan's well. It is necessary to go quite far inland to cross the river Dysynni. Pathways are usually upon the slopes; there was little level, firm ground near the shore since the sea, in very early times – but within mankind's memory – over-ran the land. We can imagine the company, at the end of the day, listening to old stories about the submerging of Gwyddno's land, and the drowning of Teithi Hen's kingdom between St David's and Ireland and how no one escaped but Teithi Hen and his horse, or of the flat, fruitful kingdom of Helig ap Glannawg between Ceredigion and Bardsey, extending as far as Aberdyfi and Llŷn. It did not trouble the travellers that these could all be different versions of the same tradition; the names of the characters and the location of stories well known in many countries are surprisingly interchangeable.

Llangelynnin church would be even smaller than it is today. A path called the Black Road could be seen leading to the Mawddach estuary. Since the coastline has changed and the sea has gained in the course of centuries, a section of twelfth century marshy strand could be under water today. It was by boat, higher up the estuary, that Giraldus Cambrensis and his company crossed. There was a ford nearer the sea, but one had to wait for the tide to ebb before venturing across; according to the survey made in 1562, it was considered a very dangerous place.

In the days of the pilgrims, there was not even a village on the north side of the estuary (where Barmouth stands today); as late as 1565 there were only four houses. By that time a sandy promontory stretched from the southern shore, narrowing the estuary, and the inhabitants rowed travellers across.

The ancient and important church of Llanaber stands a little to the north; parts of the present building belong to the period before 1200. Close by, on the shore, buried a little below today's high tide mark, two tombstones dating from *c.* 500 were discovered, one commemorating AETERNUS and AETERNA, and the other CAELEXTIS MONEDORIX.

In the thirteenth century, an Irishman called Osbwrn settled in the district. According to the story, Gruffudd, one of the sons of Ednyfed Fychan (Llywelyn the Great's steward) had to flee to Ireland because he was too friendly with Joan, Llywelyn's wife. After Llywelyn's death in 1240, he returned and Osbwrn Wyddel (the Irishman) was one of his followers. Osbwrn settled in this area – his name was on the list of parish tax-payers 1293-4 – and became the progenitor of several noble families. In October 1391, his great-grandson, Gruffudd ap Llywelyn ap Cynwrig, obtained a licence from the Pope allowing him and his descendants to celebrate mass and hold other religious services at the Hospice of the Virgin Mary, between the river Mawddach and Artro strand, 'where the tide flows and ebbs twice a day as far as the mountains which are opposite the sea,' according to the Latin document. There would be a hospice here, i.e. a lodging house where travellers in difficulty could stay. This, probably, was the old place called Egryn; it did not belong to any religious order.

On towards Llanddwywe and Llanenddwyn, where there were three wells, named after Enddwyn, Mary and Patrick. Was the last one so named through being associated with Sarn Badrig (Patrick's Causeway), the rocky ridge that stretches out to the sea, along which, according to tradition, St Patrick used to walk to and from Ireland?

Sections of very early paths are still visible in the area. First, there is the Sarn Hir (Long Causeway), leading from where the river Artro was crossed to where the village of Pen-sarn stands today. Then there are parts of old tracks near Llandanwg and at Llanfair. There was neither a town nor even the remains of a castle at Harlech before 1284, yet early native sagas associated Bendigeidfran and his family with the rock, sagas of which Edward I was aware; one of the towers of the castle he built was called Tŵr Bronwen (Bronwen's Tower). 'Bronwen', notice: according to the version of the story familiar to Siôn Phylip, the 'small swarthy poet' from Mochras close by, who was drowned when crossing home by boat from Pwllheli in 1620, the princess was 'Bronwen, daughter of the big king', not Branwen, sister of the enormous Bendigeidfran, as in the account preserved in the second branch of the Mabinogi. Variations of this type on a legend handed down in written form are certain proof of an earlier oral tradition.

The sea was very much nearer in the Middle Ages. When the castle was built at Harlech, the sea washed the rock; even on Speed's map, 1610, the river Dwyryd flowed past the foot of the rock. In the days of the pilgrims, Morfa Harlech – the flatland extending away from the castle – did not exist. The old paths kept

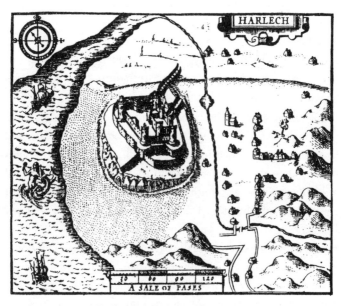

Harlech on Speed's Map, 1610.

to the hillsides as far as Talsarnau, where, at low tide, it was possible to cross the Traeth Bach (Little Strand) in more than one place, as the name Talsarnau (the end of the causeways, fording-places) implies. The river Dwyryd flowed much nearer the village than it does today; before *c.* 1825 it flowed on the southern side of Ynys Giftan. To have to follow up the river as far as the Felenrhyd to cross would add considerably to the journey.

Some of the pilgrims at Tywyn may have decided to turn eastwards and aim for the Roman road leading from Pennal to Tomen-y-mur. For many, many miles they would face a mountainous, desolate expanse; when they crossed the river Wnion, there would be only a few houses where Dolgellau stands today. In 1198-9 the Cistercians, the White Monks, founded an abbey, Cymer Abbey, near the confluence (Welsh *cymer*) of the rivers Wnion and Mawddach, across the river Mawddach from Llanelltyd church; welcome, lodging and rest could be obtained there, before facing miles of solitude once more, then over the marshy Trawsfynydd plain to reach Tomen-y-mur.

Tomen-y-mur was an important road junction. The road to the east led through Cwm Prysor towards Bala; another crossed the Migneint, went past the Maidens' Lake and the Graves of the Men of Ardudwy, along Sarn-y-ddual to Dolwyddelan and the Conwy valley; yet another led to Segontium. Should pilgrims from different localities happen to meet here, there would be much talking and telling of old tales.

It was here that Lleu and his wife, Blodeuwedd, settled. Before long Blodeuwedd turned unfaithful; she fell in love with Gronw Pebyr, lord of Penllyn, and managed to get her husband to reveal the secret of how he could be killed. But when Lleu was struck in his side with the specially prepared spear, he turned into an eagle and flew away. Eventually, Gwydion discovered him, and having restored him to his true form and complete health, both came to avenge the wrong, condemning Gronw to the same death as he had intended for Lleu. The slate Gronw held to protect his side against the thrust was of no avail; the lance pierced through the stone and killed him. That stone, with the hole through it, is still to be seen on the banks of the river Cynfal, and a farm close by bears the name Llech Ronw (Gronw's Stone). Blodeuwedd and her maids fled, in so much fear that they walked backwards, and the maids fell into a lake. 'The Maidens' Lake' is on the right as you come down the Migneint. Blodeuwedd herself was turned into an owl, a bird that strikes fear into many local inhabitants to this day.

"No!" someone would intervene, "that is not how the Maidens' Lake got its name." At one time, eligible maidens were scarce in Ardudwy, and a number of local young men went over to the Vale of Clwyd in search of wives. They found sweethearts without any difficulty, and set off back home, each with his chosen maiden riding pillion with him. But the young men of the Vale of Clwyd became furious, galloped after them and caught up with them by the lake on the Migneint. Fierce was the fighting. The Vale of Clwyd men were victorious; the Ardudwy men were all killed and buried there, and, in their distress, the maidens threw themselves into the lake and died. The names, the Maidens' Lake and the Graves of the Men of Ardudwy, testify to the truth of all this.

The Romans built a fort here, 'Mons Heriri'. The usual

name for the place in old pedigree books was 'Tomen Ynyr' (Ynyr's Mound), as if connecting the place with a Roman called Honorius. In 1097, king William Rufus erected a mound and castle within the fort; Mur Castell (Castle Wall) became another name for the place. All kinds of stories were connected with Tomen-y-mur.

One road led to the Felenrhyd, where the fight between Gwydion and Pryderi took place; Gwydion was the victor, Pryderi was killed and buried there. The name indicates there was a ford across the river Dwyryd here, before arriving at the Traeth Bach, where the two ways from Tywyn meet.

If crossing the Dwyryd estuary at Traeth Bach was dangerous, crossing the estuary of the river Glaslyn and the Traeth Mawr (Large Strand) was decidedly very much worse. It is difficult for us today to visualise the district as it was before the Portmadoc Cob was built early in the nineteenth century. The tide reached as far as Aberglaslyn bridge, and large tracts of the land between it and the sea, if not underwater, would be too marshy for the unfamiliar to travel. An arm of the sea also extended towards Penmorfa, with a ferry across. Along the Minffordd Fords was considered the best place to cross the Traeth Mawr; although the water was wider here, it was not so deep, and the river bed was harder and easier to ford. Having crossed, one aimed for Llidiard Ysbyty (the Hospice Gate), a welcome indication of a building where travellers could rest, and on the return journey wait for suitable crossing conditions.

Should there be travellers from Beddgelert here they would be sure to relate, with pride and admiration, the story of Gelert, the exceptionally graceful and swift hound that Princess Joan, king John's daughter, brought with her when she married Llywelyn the Great, a dog that could kill stags on its own. One day, having chased a big, strong stag all day, the two fought so furiously in the valley where the abbey stood that they killed one another, in the presence of the princess. In her sorrow, Joan had the dog buried honourably, and the place was called Bedd Gelert (Gelert's Grave). Experienced travellers and professional pilgrims would be familiar with an international popular tale, well known from the Far East and across Europe: the story of how a faithful, domestic animal killed a rapacious, wild animal that tried to attack the master's baby son. While they fought, the cradle was overturned, and the dog was spattered with blood; the master, thinking it had killed the baby, drew his sword and killed the dog. Too late, he discovered his child unhurt, and the dead body of the beast close by. By mid fifteenth century, this story too had become attached to Llywelyn the Great and was being told to explain the place-name, Bedd Gelert.

The remains of a paved road could be seen between the Hospice Gate and Penmorfa. This could be followed as far as Dolbenmaen, then it turned left for Llangybi and its healing well, where there was a stone marked with a cross, of the type seen on the northern route, indicating the pilgrim way. Afterwards, the path aimed for the coast on the left.

An alternative way would be to follow the coastline to Cricieth (Crug-caith, the rock of the bondsmen). Cricieth could boast of a castle before the days of Edward I, and it is presumed there was a church here, dedicated to a now unknown saint, before it was rededicated to St Catherine. Cricieth, an open town, developed very slowly. The castle was destroyed by

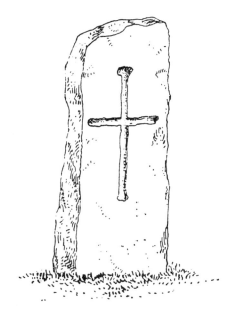

The Llangybi Cross.

Owain Glyndŵr in 1404, it was not repaired and the garrison was removed.

On again to Abererch and St Cawrdaf's church. According to folk tradition, he was known by three names: Cawrdaf, Cynfarch and Cadfarch, and was one of the seven saintly cousins who went to Rome to pray for rain, none having fallen for three years.

> Dewi a Chybi achubant – beunydd,
>
> Dwyn Beuno yn warant,
>
> Dingad, Cynfarch a barchant,
>
> A Deiniol a Seiriol sant.

[Dewi and Cybi save daily, they took Beuno as a warrant, Dingad and Cynfarch they respect, and the saintly Deiniol and Seiriol.] Folk tradition paid no heed to the fact that they were not all contemporaries. According to the story, the first drop of rain fell on Cadfarch's book, and, said he, "Bid co' gennych, wyrda, mai ar fy llyfr i y disgynnodd y defnyn cyntaf." ["Remember, good men, that it was on my book the first drop fell," and they replied, "Co-wrda".] Thus he obtained three names: Cynfarch, Cadfarch and Cawrdaf, which, according to folk wisdom, are all variations on 'co-wrda'. Cawrdaf's chair can be seen in the rock close by.

When someone had desired his body to be buried on Bardsey, it is said that the bearers would rest here with the coffin. (Was it folk wisdom again that misinterpreted the place-name and tried to turn Abererch (estuary of the river Erch) into Abereirch (estuary of coffins)?) It is believed that pilgrims who died on the journey have been buried here. It was a particular place to pray for a safe crossing to Bardsey.

Pwllheli town had been well established before the days of Edward I. It, too, like Nefyn, was ravaged by Glyndŵr, but Pwllheli managed to revive. The wise men of past centuries tried to associate the name with Helig ap Glannawg, whose realm was drowned, and maintained that Pwllhelig was the correct form of the place-name. Further west there was the chance to stay at Plas Penyberth.

Perhaps a few pilgrims would be eager to cross to the eastern St Tudwal's Isle, about a mile away. In the thirteenth century, there was a small priory here, where pilgrims would be welcomed.

Cawrdaf's Chair

Back on the mainland, there were two wells at Llanengan; to be healed it was necessary to bathe in one and drink from the other. On again to Porth Neigwl with its treacherous bay, then visit the Saint's well, before crossing the Rhiw Mountain. Over on the other side, at Llanfaelrhys, there was another healing well, where they could rest and recover before arriving at Aberdaron.

Chapter 7

Over the Perilous Sound

HAVING ARRIVED AT UWCHMYNYDD or Aberdaron, the pilgrims would be very glad of a respite. But the respite could become wearisome: although Bardsey Island is only some two and a half miles away, they often had to wait for favourable weather to cross as the sound is so exceedingly treacherous. To make matters worse, it was not always safe for pilgrims to land there, the island being an easy target for pirates. On Saturday, 6 May 1346, a thief, called J Bannerburg, visited Bardsey with two boats and thirty armed men. The abbot complained to the Chamberlain of Gwynedd that he and the canons had to bar themselves in the monastery, and the thieves took all the food and drink, as well as many other things, causing great harm to the inhabitants of the monastery.

The poet Hywel Rheinallt (*fl.c.* 1487-1500) implied that the monastery was in need of defence. On behalf of the abbot of Bardsey, he addressed a poem to Sir Siôn Elis and Owain Eutun of Maelor asking for bows:

> Saethau i'm plas a weithir,
> Nid hawdd cael bwâu i'n tir.
> Ni chair, fe gair a fo gwell,
> Hanner coed yn nhir Cadell.

[Although they could make arrows, it was not easy to get bows here. There were no trees worth while in the land of Cadell (i.e. on monastery land), though there was better treasure to be obtained.] In his elegy on Rhys Carreg, who was buried on Bardsey (who had possibly been killed in a skirmish there), the same poet mentions a scuffle with the men of Dublin.

Court Farm, Aberdaron, was excused from paying tithe on condition that free lodging could be obtained there for those waiting for the opportunity to cross. According to tradition, pilgrims also stayed at a house in Aberdaron where Y Gegin Fawr stands today.

Naturally, pilgrims would turn to Aberdaron church to worship and pray. This was the principal church in Llŷn, and it is quite possible the offertory money left by pilgrims helped its development. Until the early sixteenth century, it would only have been about half its present size. The north aisle and the west door end were built in the twelfth century, and the church was extended eastwards in the fourteenth or fifteenth century. The south aisle was added in the sixteenth century, with an arcade of five bays connecting the two aisles.

To continue their devotion during their long wait, pilgrims would wander to the small chapels in the area. One would be the chapel on Anelog Mountain, where there had been a clas at least from the beginning of the sixth century; by praying there they could expect the priest Veracius and the priest Senacus, buried in the vicinity with a multitude of brothers, to intercede on their behalf. To the north would be Odo's Chapel, then Cwmdyli Chapel, and Cadell's Church, referred to by Hywel Rheinallt, a church and three chapels of which there are no visible remains today. Even more important, there was the chapel near the shore, by St Mary's well, away at the far end of the peninsula, not far from Y Maen Melyn; although washed by the tide twice daily, the water in the well was always fresh. Could this be an instance of rededicating the well of a local saint? Most likely, pilgrims visited the site generations before the cult of the Virgin Mary reached this area. Mediaeval people believed Mary had special power to protect those facing dangers on the deep sea; she was sometimes addressed as 'Mary Virgin of the Sea', an idea and name that possibly developed by connecting the Latin form of her name, *Maria*, with the Latin word for 'sea', *mare*. It is said that bodies to be buried on Bardsey were brought here to await a favourable crossing.

Some poets experienced dangerous adventures while trying to cross the Bardsey Sound. 'I set out from Porth y Meudwy (the hermit's Harbour),' said Tomas Celli (fl. *c*. 1470-90), when he and his fellow travellers were going to the island where great miracles occur. But, poor wretches; the waves were like mountains and the sea came against them from every direction, 'Three seas united into one, exceedingly great force'.

> Gweddïais i, gweddus oedd,
> Rhag marw yn rhwygo moroedd.

[I prayed; it was fitting to do so, not to die tearing the seas.] Having managed to reach land, 'I sought nothing but heaven for my soul,' was his cry.

The experience of Rhys Llwyd ap Rhys ap Rhicert (*fl.c.* 1450), a poet from Ceredigion, was even more terrifying:

> Euthum i fad dduw Sadwrn,
> Fel yr aeth, ysywaeth, swrn.

Oferedd im gyfeiriaw,
Anllad Rys, i Enlli draw.
Mordwyodd, mawr eu duad,
Tonnau o bell tua'n bad;
Neidio o'r bad annedwydd,
A chwarae dawns, och o'r dydd!...
Sef gwnaeth ton dalgron y dydd
Torri'r llyw, taro'r llywydd.

[I entered a boat on Saturday, as did a good number, worse luck. It was foolish of me to direct irresponsible Rhys to Bardsey yonder. Waves (great was their appearance) from afar tore into our boat. The unlucky boat leapt and played a dance; woe to the day. A round high wave that day broke the rudder, struck the helmsman.] It was advised that some of the group should be cast into the sea, the poet being one of them, but the boatman forbade that.

Pan oedd fwyaf arnaf fi
Drwm feddwl draw am foddi,
Mwy am dir oedd fy hiraeth
Na mab am ei ddynion maeth.
Cilio dydd cyn cael diddos,
Difawyd ni, dyfod nos;
Dyn ni welai dan wyliad
Dor ei law, neu dir ei wlad....
Mynnwn ar ben y mynydd
Fy mod, cyn dyfod y dydd...
Gwaedd fawr, fel gweddi a fu,
A roesom ar yr Iesu,
Ar unwaith rhoes ŵyr Anna
Wawr ddydd, ac felly'r oedd dda.

[When the thought of drowning weighed heaviest on me, my longing for land was greater than that of a son for those who nurtured him. The day receded before we found shelter, we were destroyed, night had come. A man could not see, when looking, the palm of his hand nor the land of his country ... I wished I were on top of the mountain before day came ... We gave a great shout, like a prayer it was, to Jesus. At once Anna's grandson gave the dawn of day, and so it was well.] But where were they?

> Cael o'r braidd, diwladaidd lwyth,
>
> O bu rwystr, Aberystwyth.

[The bold load reached, with difficulty, in spite of hindrances, Aberystwyth.] They landed there,

> A'n heneidiau'n annedwydd,
>
> I ben traeth, heb enaid rhydd.

[With our souls wretched, to the shore, with no free soul.] i.e. they had not been freed of their sins. The poet looked pitiful:

> Ni wyddid pa un oeddwn;
>
> 'Pwy, pwy', meddynt hwy, 'yw hwn?'

[They did not know which one I was, 'Who? Who?' they said, 'is this?'] He was so feeble that he vowed,

> Ni chair myned dan chwarae
>
> I Enlli mwy, yn lle mae;
>
> Doed hithau, da y tuthir,
>
> Ynys deg, yn nes i dir!

[There will be no going thoughtlessly to Bardsey any more, where it now is. May it, fair isle, it travels well, come nearer the land.]

Despite all the troubles of the journey, Tomas Celli believed the benefits of the island far outweighed all the dangers. He marvelled at the fine, beautiful windows of coloured glass, and praised the abbot 'with his golden white hand' for his generosity, and the prior for his learning, 'his pure Latin'.

Like the poet Meilyr, in the second quarter of the twelfth century, Hywel ap Dafydd ab Ieuan ap Rhys (*fl.* 1450-80) desired to end his days there:

> Mi af i lunio fy medd
> I'r ynys oddi ar Wynedd.

[I shall go to form my grave to the island off the coast of Gwynedd.] In his poem he includes the old belief that the twenty thousand saints crossed over together. In order to sustain them, the abbot, Lleuddad, milked a cow over the well and the water turned into milk to feed them. They left their staffs on top of a hill and a miracle happened:

> Tyfasan' fel twf Foesen
> O anian pridd yn un pren,
> Pob un yn llwyn yn dwyn dail...

[They grew like Moses's growth, because of the nature of the soil, into one tree, each one a shrub bearing leaves...] It is here that one obtains a clean soul and pardon, and from here everyone goes to heaven.

But things could be different, unfortunately. In the second half of the fifteenth century, a little harmless jesting took place between two poets, Dafydd Llwyd of Mathafarn and Llywelyn ap Gutyn. Dafydd advised Llywelyn to go to Bardsey for the good of his soul. But poor Llywelyn:

Anŵraidd it fy ngyrru
Yn llaw ddiawl i Enlli ddu;
Man ni cheid, er eich mwyn chwi,
Na hybarch farch na hobi.
'Drinc âl,' meddai mab Alis,'
'Brwder, sit, eat bread and sis.'
Oer rhag llaw y'm croesawodd,
Abad heb roi'n rhad un rhod.

[It was wretched of you to send me in the hand of the devil to black Bardsey; where no one got, for your sake, either a good horse or a hobby. 'Drink all,' said Alice's son, 'Brother, sit, eat bread and cheese.' It was coldly the abbot welcomed me, without giving free any gift.] He did not receive a gift of any kind, not even a hobby, the smallest kind of falcon used to hunt larks and small birds. Despite the foreign language, it is not likely that the abbot was an Englishman; 'son of Alice' was a derisive term, implying the fraud and deceit of Alice Rhonwen, Hengist's daughter, who had been responsible for the treachery of the long knives in the time of Gwrtheyrn.

Someone told another poet, Deio ab Ieuan Du from Creuddyn, Ceredigion (*fl.* 1460-80), that Madog ap Madog, abbot of Bardsey, was an extremely generous man, fond of poets. Deio composed an elegy to him, and hired a boat to go to Bardsey, but all he received from the miserly abbot was a little bread and cheese and buttermilk, he having expected appetising, lavish feasts. He then composed a poem, ridiculing the abbot:

Madog Amhadog, gwr hynaws – ei dŷ
Wedi'i dôi â hengaws,
Ac eilio'i nen â hengaws,
A chau ei logel â chaws.

> Bragod ni cheisioddd ond briwgaws, – y bore
>> A berwi maidd a chaws;
>> A chanol dydd mŷdd meiddgaws,
>> A phrynhawn ni a gawn gaws.

[Madog ap Madog, a genial man, his house roofed with old cheese, his ceiling woven with old cheese, and his chest closed with cheese. He sought no bragget but broken cheese in the morning and boiled whey and cheese; and midday a large vessel of cheese-whey, and in the afternoon we had cheese.] Every part of the building – the roof, the ceiling and walls – were all made of cheese, according to the poet. The only drink was a large vessel of whey, the thick, sour liquid left after taking the cheese out of it. Goats' milk, honey-cheese and whey were everywhere; every dish on Christmas day was of cheese, even the wine. The miserly abbot churned and reaped, milked and coagulated, to avoid having to pay anyone wages; he could feed a hundred without a cook, butler or server, without even a spit. Exaggeration was an obvious figure of speech with the poets, but there is reason to believe that life on Bardsey was often destitute.

In 1538, when a survey was made of the abbey's possessions, it was stated that the land had never been cultivated and ploughed, mainly because of the damage done by the hordes of rabbits there. In a jest poem, sometime during the second half of the fourteenth century, Iolo Goch mentions, mockingly, that Ithel Ddu had gone to Bardsey to hunt rabbits for a thousand saints. As early as 1291, the sale of rabbits, for their meat and for their skins, brought in a welcome income for the Augustinian Canons. The skins were in great demand. We today complain how cold some churches are, but think of those of the Middle Ages: several of the large churches and monasteries were in the course of construction, many windows unglazed, and no provision at all for heating. The only way to keep fairly warm was to wear a fur coat, and, over it, to hide it, a *superpellicium*, 'over garment of skin', a term that gave us the English word 'surplice' (and the mediaeval Welsh word *siorplys*). Cloaks and hoods were also lined with fur. The noble and the rich could afford ermine or squirrel; the less fortunate had to be satisfied with rabbit skins.

But it was not to enjoy sumptuous feasts that people went to Bardsey; the pardons and miracles were the attractions. When the monastery was dissolved, the Bodwrda family of Aberdaron got hold of an old document, 'Possessions and Privileges of Bardsey Abbey.' A Latin copy, in the hand of Wiliam Bodwrda (1593-1660) has survived. The document testifies that the pardons and privileges were given to the abbot of Bardsey by the high Popes of Rome, and that they were attainable to all who believed in Christ if they were penitent and performed penance and confession, and for their own benefit contributed or sent a gift of the goods that God had given them, in honour of the twenty thousands saints and to support the work of the monastery of the Blessed Virgin Mary on Bardsey Island generally called the Rome of Britain in the diocese of Bangor. Christ continues to show miracles: gives hearing to the deaf, voice to the dumb, sight to the blind, walking ability to the lame, sanity to the insane, and to those in peril on the sea guidance to a safe harbour; all this in response to the beseeching of the saints Cybi, David, Cadfan, Daniel [Deiniol], Seiriol, Beuno, Cawrdaf, to the glory of God and the Blessed Virgin

NLW Manuscript N 1559B
(printed with the permission of the National Library of Wales).

Mary and the twenty thousand saints.' The section listing the pardons is incomplete.

Mention was made earlier (p.p.45–6) of the pilgrim, having arrived at the end of his journey, completing the penance. While clearing old remains, or digging foundations for new buildings, objects that could have been part of an offering have been found: part of a bishop's crosier of silver, a peculiar key that could have been a ring and a seal, 45 pieces of gold, a silver model of an arm and hand, a certain indication that someone was seeking, or giving thanks for recovery of those limbs.

A copy of the 'Absolution from Pain and Punishment' is also to be found in Wiliam Bodwrda's handwriting:

> Our Lord Jesus Christ forgives thee, and I [the priest] by the authority of our Sacred Mother the Church, entrusted to me from the apostolic seat, absolve thee from every bond of excommunication, sentence of inhibition, every irregularity and prohibition imposed on thee, I shall restore thee to the sacraments of the Church, and with the same authority I completely free thee from all thy sins, confessed or forgotten, and from the punishment due to thee for thy transgressions. In the name of the Father, and of the Son, and of the Holy Ghost.

It is almost certain that the monastery's income was always small, and that it diminished regularly towards the end of the period. When the account was made before the dissolution, only £2 a year was being obtained in offerings. By that time, undertaking pilgrimages was coming to an end. Many felt the journey to Bardsey was too dangerous, and centres easier to

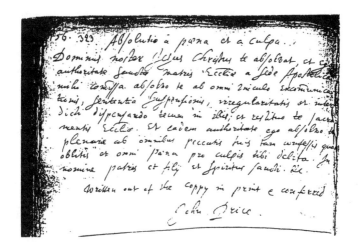

NLW Manuscript N 1559B
(printed with the permission of the National Library of Wales.
A person called John Price was rector of Bofean 1613–8, and of
Mellteyrn and Botwnnog 1618–?).

reach had become popular. With the growth in wealth and ready money, it is not rash to suggest that to give a sum of money to the Church could act as a substitute for a pilgrimage; a change in the country's economy had begun before the change in the country's religion.

According to local tradition, Bardsey Abbey had a good library, and a large tower with six bells; tradition also maintains that the bells were removed to Llanengan church. The abbey was dissolved *c.* 1537. There is no reference to the number of monks, but it mentions a small abbey or priory, a church with a tower, rooms and barns, orchards and gardens. They were left to fall into ruin; by 1846 only the thirteenth century ruined tower remained standing. Part of a cross and a stone with a cross engraved on it are the only relics.

And yet, old beliefs and traditions dragged on. When Huw ap Rhisiart of Bodwrda died, some time after the dissolution, for the good of his soul he was buried on Bardsey; as the poet Wiliam Llŷn (*ob.* 1580) stated in an elegy to him:

> Modd yw i gael maddeuaint,
> Mae'ch bedd lle bu senedd saint.

[It is a means to obtain forgiveness; your grave is where once there was a senate of saints.]

The Old Faith did not end all at once in Llŷn and Eifionydd; some of the families remained faithful for a long time. Three of the sons of Owain ap Gruffudd of Plas-du, Llanarmon, crossed to the continent in order to foster and serve it. Huw Owen (1538–1618), the arch-plotter, as he was called, worked as a spy for the king of Spain for forty years; Robert was a Catholic priest, and Siôn (*ob.c.* 1595) studied law at Douai, while Tomas, the eldest brother, at home at Plas-du, supported them with the tithes of Aberdaron. When Dr Elis Prys, Plasiolyn, and Nicholas Robinson, bishop of Bangor, in 1578 searched Plas-du, Madryn, Cefnamwlch and Pennarth, on behalf of the government, they found letters, and reported, 'We take it that although the said Robert [Owen] speaketh of trifles he meaneth other things of more importance.'

Robert Gwyn, second son of Siôn Wyn ap Tomas Gruffudd of Penyberth, who conducted a mission for the Old Faith in Llŷn and other parts of Wales during the last quarter of the sixteenth century, was the author of several texts promoting Roman Catholicism. It was in a cave at Rhiwledyn, on the

Little Orme, that *Y Drych Cristianogawl* was printed in 1585, stating on the title-page it was printed at Rhotomagi (Rouen).

Among government papers there is a short piece that belongs to the very end of the sixteenth century – possibly 1599 – instructing a pilgrim how to go to Bardsey. At 'Puhley' (Pwllheli) 'a port town', he was to ask for Wm John, who would direct him to 'Penyberts' (Penyberth), a mile away; there he was to desire Griffin Wyn (Robert Gwyn's brother) or his son John, to guide him to Bardsey. The longing to rest in the deep peace of Bardsey remained.

Bardsey in 1823.

Also published by Y Lolfa:

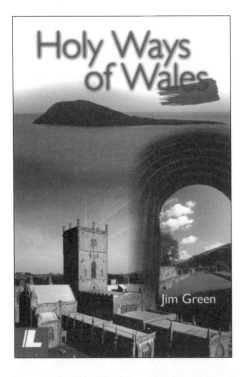

During the Middle Ages, Wales was famous for her pilgrimage sites and routes. After Rome, St. David's and Bardsey Island counted as equal in holiness to Santiago de Compostella. This book retraces the holy ways of Wales, pointing out significant places and buildings.

£6.95
ISBN 0 86243 519 6

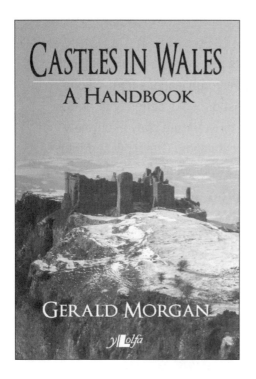

A comprehensive introduction to the castles of Wales, with detailed guides to 70 castles. Covers the contemporary historical significance of castles, the military and political background, building stone castles and mottes and ringworks, the builders, and castles of the Welsh princes.

£7.95

ISBN 9 78184771 031 4

This book is just one of a whole range of
Welsh-interest publications from Y Lolfa.
For a full list of books currently in print,
send now for your free copy of our new
full colour catalogue. Or simply surf into
our website

www.ylolfa.com

for secure on-line ordering.

TALYBONT CEREDIGION CYMRU SY24 5AP
e-bost ylolfa@ylolfa.com
gwefan www.ylolfa.com
ffôn (01970) 832 304
ffacs 832 782